The Credit Crunch

Colin Hynson

W

FRANKLIN WATTS

LONDON•SYDNEY

First published in 2009
by Franklin Watts

Copyright © Franklin Watts 2009

Franklin Watts
338 Euston Road
London NW1 3BH

Franklin Watts Australia
Level 17/207 Kent Street
Sydney, NSW 2000

Editor: Jeremy Smith
Design: Simon Borrough
Art director: Jonathan Hair

Picture credits: Peter Bennett/Alamy: 31.
Kanwarjit Singh Boparai/Alamy: front cover b,
16. Francesco Carta fotografo/Shutterstock:
front cover t, 30. Jon Challicom/Alamy: 29.
Humberto Olarte Cupas/Alamy: 14. Dmitrijs
Dmitrijevs/Shutterstock: 12. Jeremy
Edwards/istockphoto: 18b. Eurostyle
Graphics/Alamy: 35. Feverpitch/Shutterstock:
20. Frontpage/Shutterstock: 25b. Wolfgang
Kaehler/Alamy: 32. Jonathan
Larsen/Shutterstock: 9. David Levenson/Alamy:
26. Ryan McGinnis/Alamy: 15. MEPL/Alamy:
11. Mirrorpix/Alamy: 38. Keith Morris/Alamy:
8. Sigurdur Jokull Olafsson/Alamy: 36, 37.
David Pearson/Alamy: 10. Duncan
Phillips/Alamy: 34. Reuters/Corbis: 22, 23.
Rough Guides/Alamy: 39. Phillip Scalia/Alamy:
40. Joseph Sohm/Alamy: 19, 33. Della
Spyridoule /Alamy: 21. Duncan Hale-
Sutton/Alamy: 17. Konstantin
Sutyagin/Shutterstock: 28. Rainer
Unkel/vario/Alamy: 25t. Jim West/Alamy: 18c.
Wrangler/Shutterstock: 13.

A CIP catalogue record for this book
is available from the British Library.

Dewey number: 339.5'3-dc22

ISBN 978 0 7496 9229 2

Printed in China

Franklin Watts is a division of
Hachette Children's Books,
an Hachette Livre UK company
www.hachettelivre.co.uk

Contents

The Financial World Explained

The origins of the credit crunch and the economic troubles that the world is facing can be found in the complex world of finance. These are the finances of individuals, businesses of all sizes and even of governments. If the credit crunch is to be understood properly then words and phrases such as credit, interest rates, stock markets, and mortgages need to be explored first.

Mortgages

One of the biggest purchases that anybody will make in their whole lives is buying a home to live in. Since homes are very expensive, most people will borrow money in the form of a mortgage. This money is lent by a financial institution, such as a bank, to help somebody buy a property. The loan is paid back over several years with interest. A percentage is added to the original loan so that the home buyer always pays back more than he or she initially borrowed. The borrower has to carry on paying the loan and the interest until it is all paid off. If the borrower cannot pay back the mortgage then the bank can foreclose on, or take possession of, the property. The level of interest is called the interest rate. Interest rates are calculated in different ways. If the lender thinks the loan is risky then they will make the interest rate higher, so that they will make less of a loss if the loan cannot be paid.

When people buy a home they have to find something that they can afford. Most people then have to find a mortgage to buy the house. They also have to make sure that they can earn enough money to pay back the mortgage.

'It is well that the people of the nation do not understand our banking and monetary system, for if they did, I believe there would be a revolution before tomorrow morning.'

Henry Ford, founder of the Ford Motor Company.

However, if financial institutions have plenty of money to lend and they want people to borrow from them then they might offer a low interest rate to attract borrowers. Lending any money that is paid back over a period of time is known as credit.

Stock Markets

There are stock markets around the world. They allow people to buy and sell shares in companies. These shares mean that the buyer then owns a part or 'share' in that company and is known as a shareholder. Companies can use money from shareholders to invest in their business. The shareholders will be entitled to a part of any profit made. Many shareholders will also make a profit by selling their shares for more than they paid for them. However, there is no guarantee that this will happen and shareholders can also lose money if the value of their shares goes down.

Central Banks

Most countries around the world have a central bank. In the USA, this is the Federal Reserve; in Britain it is the Bank of England and in China it is the People's Bank of China. These central banks are responsible for looking after the finances of the whole country, for regulating financial institutions and for lending money to banks during periods of financial crisis.

The headquarters of the Federal Reserve is called the Eccles Building and is based in Washington DC. It is close to other government buildings such as the White House.

What is the Credit Crunch?

In the last few months of 2008, the news about the world economy began to sound more gloomy. One phrase that appeared again and again was the 'credit crunch', although it has also been called a 'credit crisis' or a 'credit squeeze'. At first a 'credit crunch' only affects banks, but it eventually leads to problems in the rest of the economy. This could then become a recession or even a depression in the economy.

When an economy goes into recession, there are more people are all chasing a smaller number of jobs. This can give rise to queues of people all looking for work.

Credit Crunches

When a bank, or any other financial institution, lends money then it has to be confident that the money will eventually be paid back along with any interest on the loan. When the economy is doing well, then banks are willing to lend money because they believe that it will be paid back. However, what happens is that many banks become too confident about lending money. This means that loans are given to those who are more likely to have difficulty paying the money back. When the economy begins to weaken, and people find it harder to make money, then many find it hard to repay their loans. Banks react to this by suddenly reducing the amount of credit that they are willing to lend. This creates problems for individuals and businesses that need to borrow money.

THOUGHT BOX

Many people have said that there should be more rules to make sure that banks lend money in a responsible way. Do you think that banks should have tighter controls over their lending? What problems do you think adopting such a policy might lead to?

A queue of men outside a job centre in 1930s Britain.

An Economic Downturn

Economies grow when people spend more money and more things are produced for people to buy. If a credit crunch carries on for too long then people and businesses will have less money to spend. In the end this will lead to a recession. A recession is when economies start to shrink. People spend less money and less goods are produced. This leads to unemployment. People without a job do not have as much money so they spend even less. A credit crunch is just one of many causes of a recession. A severe or prolonged recession is often called a depression.

'A **recession** is when your neighbor loses his job. A depression is when you lose yours.'

Ronald Reagan speaking in 1980 during the US Presidential campaign

The Good Times

Economies around the world often go through major changes called economic cycles. For a few years a country will enjoy a period of prosperity and people will have a good standard of living. However, there are often periods when countries are less prosperous and may even go through a recession. This is called a 'correction' in the economy. Eventually, things improve again. To understand the present economic difficulties it is important to know something about the 'good times' that came before.

THOUGHT BOX

Do you think that periods of prosperity make up for 'corrections' in the economic cycle? Do you think the two balance each other out?

During periods of prosperity then people have more money to go shopping. Shopping malls in countries from the United States to China became popular as people went to the shops to spend money.

The Consumer Boom

For the first few years of the 21st century, economies around the world were growing at a rate that had not been seen for many years. In the USA, unemployment fell from nearly 8 per cent in 1995 to around 5 per cent between 2000 and 2005. After 2001, the US economy was growing at anything between 3 and 9 per cent a year. The same was true in nearly every country in the Western world.

Built on Credit

Economic growth at the start of the 21st century was driven largely by people spending more and more money. Much of the money that they spent was in the form of money that they had borrowed. Banks and other financial institutions were happy to lend money because they were confident that it would be paid back in the end. Credit became easier to get and there was a lot of competition to offer people more and more credit.

Housing Bubbles

When an economy is doing well, then the price of property, especially homes for people to live in, begins to rise. This is because people are feeling more confident about taking on a mortgage; banks are happy to give out mortgages and interest rates are low so the amount that is paid back is lower. In the first years of the 21st century, this led to a 'housing bubble' in many countries. This means that the price of property rises at a very fast rate indeed. In 2000 in the US, an average home cost about US$200,000. Just seven years later the average price was US$320,000. In Britain many properties were increasing in value by 20 per cent per year.

As the value of property went up then this led to a boom in building. Many cities around the world saw new office blocks and homes being built at a very fast rate.

"Britain today has the lowest inflation for 30 years...Britain has had the lowest interest rates for 40 years...Britain is now enjoying the longest period of

sustained economic growth for 200 years.

And no longer the country of mass unemployment, Britain is now advancing further and faster towards full employment than at any time in our lives."

Gordon Brown, the then Chancellor of Britain, from a speech given in 2004

Reckless Lending

When looking for the origins of the current economic crisis, many people point to the rise of sub-prime lending in the USA, particularly in the areas of mortgages for houses and in obtaining credit cards. This kind of lending has been around for many years but it was only after 2001 that it was widely used. Many countries have some kind of sub-prime lending, but it was the United States that led in its popularity with both lenders and borrowers.

People who lived in the poorer parts of cities in the US were encouraged to take out sub-prime mortgages. Many of these flats would have been bought with sub-prime mortgages.

The Sub-Prime Market

Sub-prime lending was a phrase that only became well known as the financial crisis that it caused began to appear in 2007. Whenever banks or any other financial institutions lend money to somebody, they have to be sure that he or she will pay it back. Usually checks are done on the amount of money the borrower earns and whether he or she already has other debts. This is called a credit rating. If the credit rating is low, the bank may not lend money to the person because there is a high risk that they will not be able to repay the loan. It is estimated that about 25 per cent of the US population has a low credit rating.

'The main thing that innovations in the mortgage market have done over the past 30 years is to let in the

excluded:

the young, the discriminated against, the people without a lot of money in the bank to use for a down payment.'

Professor Harvey Rosen, Princeton University, USA

American cities such as Detroit and Cleveland, with large numbers of African-Americans living in them, were targeted by financial institutions offering sub-prime mortgages.

A sub-prime loan is a loan that is aimed at people with low credit rating scores. As the US economy grew, competition for loans and mortgages became more fierce, lenders began to look for new borrowers and sub-prime borrowers were targeted. These people either earned very little money or had a history of bad debts and were sometimes referred to as NINJAs (No Income, No Job or Assets). They were charged higher fees for these loans because of the extra risk. Sub-prime mortgages were given out because the lenders relied on house prices going up. This meant that if they had to foreclose then they could sell the house and make a profit.

Expanding Sub-Prime

Supporters of sub-prime mortgages said that it allowed people who would normally be excluded from getting a normal mortgage to buy their own homes. Many of the sub-prime borrowers came from communities that were traditionally poorer (and so would have a poor credit rating). African-Americans and Hispanic Americans began to buy their own homes using sub-prime mortgages. By 2006, one in five mortgages in the US were sub-prime.

The Crisis Begins

Many people who took out mortgages feared that they could not keep up with their payments. They were forced to sell or face losing their homes.

Sub-prime lending, particularly sub-prime mortgages, depend on several things for their success. House prices need to carry on going up, interest rates on the loans need to stay low so that it is easier to pay them back, and the economy as a whole needs to be growing so that people are earning money. If any of these things start to go wrong, then there is a risk that sub-prime borrowers will not be able to pay off their loans. By August 2007, it was becoming clear that something was going wrong.

Payment Difficulties

In order to attract people to take up a sub-prime loan, many lenders had offered an initial lower interest rate on any loan. This meant that for the first two or three years it was easier to pay off any loan. This initial offer meant that many borrowers took on large mortgages in the belief that they could pay them off. However, at the end of that period these borrowers were then moved on to a higher interest rate. Suddenly, many people found that they were having great difficulty keeping up the repayments. This was a real problem because some people took a sub-prime mortgage even though they already owned their homes. They used this money to buy other things such as cars or holidays. In Britain, many people got into payment difficulties not because their mortgages were sub-prime but because they had simply taken out too large a mortgage. Until recently some people were getting 100 per cent mortgages or even 110 per cent mortgages. As long as house prices continued upwards this was not a problem. However, people are now beginning to have difficulties paying these mortgages.

At the same time, house price rises began to slow down and then start to fall. By September 2008, house prices in the US had fallen by 20 per cent from the peak in 2006. This caused something called negative equity. This is when the value of the house falls so much that it is worth less than the mortgage that was taken out.

Piling Up the Debt

Because more and more people were unable to keep up with their mortgages, lenders around the USA began to foreclose on the properties. They now had debts that could not be paid back and houses that could not be sold at a profit because of negative equity. Also, as mortgage lenders tried to sell these houses, prices fell even further.

The Liquidity Crisis

In order to keep money moving around the economy, banks often lent money to each other. However, as banks began to get into trouble with unpaid debts they became reluctant to lend to other banks. This was because they did not know which banks were able to pay back any money lent to them. This created something called a liquidity crisis. Banks could neither lend money to other banks nor borrow any themselves.

THOUGHT BOX

Many people took out a sub-prime mortgage so that they could spend money on something else. Do you think that people should be allowed to take out these debts if they are not going to be used to buy a house?

One of the first banks to suffer from the liquidity crisis was the British bank Northern Rock. When the bank asked the Bank of England for help their customers tried to take their money out of the bank.

northern rock

'I wanted to clear up my debts. I had quite a few credit card debts that I thought I could pay off with a mortgage...it seemed so easy at the time.'

Roger Rodriguez from Colorado, USA, interviewed by the BBC in November 2008

A Community Hit

The sub-prime crisis began to spread across the US. Communities that were worst hit were those where residents were, on the whole, poorer and with large African-American or Hispanic populations. Since 2007, some cities have seen house prices collapse and the people who live in these cities experiencing a lot of financial trouble. One of these cities is Detroit.

Detroit City

Detroit is the largest city in the state of Michigan. It has a population of about one million people. Over 80 per cent of all the people who live in Michigan are African-American. Hispanic people make up about 5 per cent of the population and about 12 per cent are white. The biggest employers in the city are three car manufacturers: General Motors, Ford and Chrysler, who between them employ 20 per cent of Detroit's working population. Many rely indirectly on these companies for their jobs.

THOUGHT BOX

What, if anything, should be done to help people in situations such as those in Detroit? If the people of Detroit are helped, then is that fair on other cities that are suffering?

This glittering skyline of Detroit hides the fact that many people in the city still work in the car industry and that there are still a lot of people living below the poverty line.

'It's sad to see what's happening here.

The longer they (estate agents) keep an empty house on their books, the higher the chances of vandalism, the chances of somebody going in and burning it up, of someone going in and stripping all the copper out. They could have squatters in there; it's happening all the time.'

Tracie Peltier, an estate agent in Detroit

House prices in Detroit have fallen so much that it has been very difficult to find any buyers. Detroit has thousands of empty properties that have simply been abandoned by their owners.

Detroit's Sub-Prime Crisis

Many people in Detroit were encouraged to take out sub-prime mortgages. These mortgages were not always used to buy houses but were used to pay off other debts or to buy luxury goods. At the start of 2007, Detroit's economy began to weaken, particularly in the car industry. This led to a rise in unemployment. Houses began to be repossessed or foreclosed on by banks and other mortgage lenders and house prices began to fall dramatically. At the start of 2008, Detroit became the repossession capital of the United States. During 2007, 5 per cent of all households in Detroit had either been repossessed or were in the early stages of repossession.

House Price Collapse

Since 2007, house prices in the US have been falling steadily. In Detroit this has become a house price collapse. Over 12,000 properties have been abandoned by their owners. They cannot keep up with their mortgage payments and they cannot sell their houses so they have simply left them. In October 2008, one three-bedroom house was on sale for US$1250. In 2001, the same house had sold for US$88,000 and two years later was sold again for US$33,000.

The Crisis Spreads

Although the sub-prime crisis appeared to hit borrowers the hardest, it also led to another crisis within the banking world. It was not just the banks that had loaned the money in the first place that were affected. Many of these financial institutions had actually sold their debts on to banks that had not been involved in sub-prime selling. The banking crisis was international. Banks from Britain, France and Germany had become part of sub-prime selling in the USA and they were hit as hard as the US banks.

The First Cracks

In 2007, as house prices in the USA began to fall and people had difficulty paying their mortgages, some financial institutions found themselves in trouble. In April 2007, a company called New Century Financial, that specialised in sub-prime mortgages, filed for bankruptcy. This meant that the company could no longer pay off the debts that it had built up from sub-prime mortgages. These debts had been bought by other banks such as Goldman Sachs and Barclays. The collapse of New Century Financial started the banking crisis.

As the sub-prime crisis spread banks and other financial institutions found that they could not pay off their debts. Even selling houses that they had foreclosed on did not help very much.

Losses Announced

Banks around the world began to announce that they had lost massive amounts of money because of the sub-prime crisis. Banks including UBS, Merrill Lynch and Citigroup revealed that they had lost billions of dollars. In September 2007, the British bank Northern Rock asked the Bank of England for financial help because of its losses. This caused a 'run on the bank', as thousands of customers tried to withdraw their money from Northern Rock. The British government had to guarantee the safety of money in the bank.

THOUGHT BOX

Do you think that banks that did not deal with sub-prime mortgages should have to suffer because of the actions of those who did?

'By Monday morning, it was clear we were bankrupt. The whole command structure had fallen. There was no direction from our bosses; they had no information to give us…I thought in the worst case scenario I would get three months' notice. What happened was that we learnt we wouldn't get paid on Friday. On the floor people were in huddles.

The scale of this is frightening.'

An anonymous Lehman Brothers employee speaking in September 2008

Losses of major banks announced in 2008

UBS	$3.4 billion
Citigroup	$40 billion
Merrill Lynch	$7.9 billion
HBOS	£1.31 billion
Bradford and Bingley	£26.7 billion
Lehman Brothers	$3.9 billion
Washington Mutual	$2.9 billion

Buying Up Banks

Some banks came close to collapse and could only survive by agreeing to be bought by one of their rivals. In March 2008, Bear Stearns was taken over by JP Morgan Chase. Six months later, the giant mortgage lender Washington Mutual was also sold to JP Morgan Chase, and Merrill Lynch was bought by the Bank of America. In the same month, the British bank Lloyds TSB took over HBOS, Britain's biggest mortgage lender. Some banks could not find buyers and collapse. In July 2008, the US mortgage lender IndyMac became bankrupt. The biggest bank to collapse was Lehman Brothers, the world's fourth-largest bank, after announcing a loss of US$3 billion in three months. All of this made the liquidity crisis even worse.

An employee of Lehman Brothers walks out of his office after being told that he has lost his job.

Government Rescue Plans

Since the 1980s, governments around the world have embraced what is called free-market economics. This means that they allowed their economies to develop without too much government interference. This worked when the world's economies were doing well. However, when economic problems begin to appear, then governments are forced to take a more active role in their economies. The credit crunch has become a huge issue for governments all over the world and many governments have acted quickly to try and soften the impact of the credit crunch.

Government Options

The possible collapse in the banking sector meant that governments had no choice but to come up with a rescue plan. If the banking sector was allowed to fail, then the impact on the rest of the economy would be huge. In order to rescue the banks, the governments have to deal with the liquidity crisis. This means that banks must become more confident about lending money to each other and to their customers. Governments could 'buy' the bad debts off the banks so that they could both lend and borrow money again. Governments could also lower interest rates. This would mean that borrowing money would become cheaper for many people. From the lenders point

The credit crunch has happened because of decisions made by banks. Do you think that they should be held responsible for these decisions and do you believe that we should help them out of a situation that they helped to create?

THOUGHT BOX

George W. Bush was US President from 2001 until 2009. He put forward the first rescue package for US banks in October 2008.

of view, a lower interest rate would mean that the borrower is more likely to pay back the loan and so there would be more confidence about lending. For borrowers, any loans taken out would be cheaper.

Because the credit crunch is global and also because so many national economies depend on each other for survival, then international co-operation between governments has also became more important. In November 2008, the leaders of the most important economies in the world met in Washington DC, and agreed to work together to fight the crisis.

The US Rescue Package

On 3 October 2008, the US House of Representatives passed a rescue package for banks in the USA that had been put forward by President George Bush. The package put aside US$700 billion of government money in order to buy the bad debts of US banks. This was a massive increase in the amount of money that the government would spend every year. It was also a controversial package because many Americans believed that their banks had got into trouble because of their own greed and so should not be helped out. Other governments have followed with their own rescue packages.

The G20 is made up of the 20 most powerful economies in the world. It met in November 2008 to discuss how to help the world's economy.

'I know some Americans have concerns about this legislation, especially about the government's role and the bill's cost... As a strong supporter of free enterprise, I believe government intervention should occur only when necessary. In this situation, action is clearly necessary.'

Former US President George W. Bush on the passing of the rescue package

Governments Take Over

In the first few decades after World War II (1939–1945), many governments nationalised important parts of their economies. Nationalisation means that these parts of the economy were taken over and run by the government. From the 1980s onwards, many of these industries were returned to private hands. It was seen as an important part of a return to free-market economics. The credit crunch has meant that governments have had to act in ways that would have been unthinkable a couple of years ago. Governments are nationalising financial institutions in order to save them.

The First Government Take-Over

The first bank to be taken over by any government was the troubled British bank, Northern Rock. Since September 2007, Northern Rock had been in crisis and the British government had been trying to find a way to rescue the bank. In February 2008, it was decided that the bank would be nationalised until the economy improved and then it could be sold back to the private sector. The nationalisation cost the British taxpayer about £55 billion. In October 2008, the British government took over 60 per cent of the Royal Bank of Scotland and 40 per cent of Lloyds TSB and HBOS. The banks received billions of pounds which they could use for lending purposes.

US Government Take-Overs

The USA has been one country that has traditionally disliked the idea of nationalising any industry. However, in September 2008, the US government took over the mortgage giants of Freddie Mac and Fannie Mae. Both companies had lost billions of dollars as house prices in the USA continued to fall. Between them these two companies had provided over half of all mortgages in the US.

'We took these actions first, to avert the financial market meltdown that would ensue from the collapse of these institutions and, second, to allow them, in the midst of overall market stress, to perform their essential role of providing mortgage finance. This conservatorship **(government ownership),** with the explicit backing of the federal government, is temporary.'

Henry Paulson, US Secretary to the Treasury

THOUGHT BOX

Government money comes from taxpayers. Should this be used to rescue banks and other financial institutions? What other options are there to protect the banks, or should they be allowed to fail?

Treasury Secretary Henry Paulson convinced President Bush that it would be a disaster for the American economy if these companies failed. It meant that the government was now responsible for US$14 billion dollars of bad debt and controlled the mortgages of millions of Americans.

The Risk of Take-Over

There is a large risk attached to governments taking over the control of some of their banks. It has cost governments billions of pounds and there is no guarantee that their actions will succeed. If the world's economies continue to slide into a deeper recession, then it might be that governments will have to spend even more money to keep these banks afloat. That will leave governments with massive debts to try to pay off.

Henry Paulson was the head of the US Treasury from 2006 until January 2009. He told President Bush that Freddie Mac and Fannie Mae had to be rescued by the government.

Freddie Mac was set up in 1970 to provide mortgages for homebuyers in the USA. It grew to be one of the biggest companies in the country before it was taken over by the government in September 2008.

Cutting Interest and Cutting Taxes

As the negative impact of the credit crunch moves from the banks into the rest of the economy and a worldwide recession gets deeper, governments are looking for ways to halt the slowdown in the economy and to start growth again. One of the ways to do this is to give people the confidence to carry on spending money. This will push up demand for goods in the shops and will then create jobs.

Cutting Interest Rates

One of the jobs of central banks such as the Federal Reserve in the USA and the Bank of England in Britain is to set the interest rate at which banks can lend to each other. Central banks do not set all interest rates, such as the interest on mortgages. That is still the decision of banks and other financial institutions.

The Bank of England Monetary Policy Committee meets every month to decide the interest rate. In recent months they have been cutting the rate in order to encourage banks to lend money.

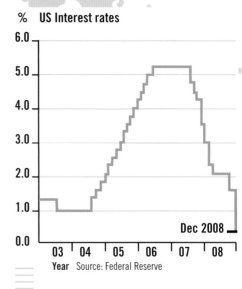

A table showing how US interest rates have changed since 2003.

In the last few months of 2008, central banks around the world began cutting their interest rates in an attempt to get banks lending money to each other and to their customers again. The aim was also to persuade these banks to cut their interest rates to their customers. In January 2009, the Bank of England cut its interest rate to 1.5 per cent. A month earlier, the Federal Reserve in the US cut their interest rate to just 0.25 per cent.

There are problems with cutting interest rates. Although it may encourage people to spend money by taking on debts, many people have said that it was debt that started the credit crunch in the first place. Because banks have debts that they need to pay off, many of them have not passed on these cuts to their customers. On top of that, low interest rates discourage people from saving money. This means that people are not putting money into banks.

Tax and Spend

Nearly all of the money that is spent by governments comes through taxes. There are many different kinds of taxes such as taxes on income and on buying goods. If governments want to encourage people to spend more money, then they can cut some of these taxes. At the end of November 2008, the British government cut the VAT rate (a tax on goods bought in shops) from 17.5 per cent to 15 per cent. In the US, the government passed a law to give back tax money to people. At the same time, many governments have increased their own spending to try and get their economies moving. Much of this money will be spent on creating new jobs or safeguarding existing jobs. However, this means that governments will be taking on a much bigger debt as they are spending more and at the same time they are getting less money in from taxes. Some people fear that this might create problems in the future as governments struggle to pay off these massive debts.

THOUGHT BOX

Some people have said that the debts that governments are creating will have to be paid off in the future by today's children. Others think that this is the only way to save the world's economy. What do you think?

'To prevent the recession deepening we need to take action to put money into the economy immediately...this reduction is the equivalent to the government

giving back

some £12 billion to consumers to boost the economy.'

Alistair Darling, the British Chancellor of the Exchequer, announcing a VAT cut on 24 November 2008

From Wall Street to Main Street

Governments around the world have taken action to protect banks and to encourage people to spend money because of the threat of a global recession in 2009. This means that economies around the world are shrinking. There will be an impact on people as jobs are lost around the world. As unemployment rises, so demand for goods falls. This creates a situation where even more jobs are lost. Many people believe that only when the problem of the credit crunch is solved will the threat of a deep recession or even a depression begin to fade away.

Causes of the Recession

There have been many recessions in the past. Every recession has had different causes. The current recession has its origins in the credit crunch. Businesses have had great difficulty getting extra money from banks because they are reluctant to give out any more loans. The threat of unemployment and falls in house prices also mean that people do not want to spend money. However, in 2008 there was another factor that made the situation worse. At the start of 2008, the prices of basic goods such as food and oil began to rise sharply. In January 2008, a barrel of oil cost US$100 (a barrel of oil is about 42 US gallons or 159 litres). The price continued to rise until July 2008 when a barrel cost about US$147. At the same time, the price of basic foods, such as rice and flour also began to rise quickly. The price of rice doubled between January and April 2008. These price rises caused riots in developing countries such as Bangladesh, Egypt and Indonesia. In richer countries, oil and food price rises meant that people had to spend more money on what are seen as essential goods. This meant that they had less money to spend on non-essential things. By the end of 2008, oil and food prices had fallen dramatically but the damage had already been done.

THOUGHT BOX

What do you think people should do in order to protect themselves from recession?

One of the main causes of the current recession was the rising price of oil. This meant the cost of petrol went up.

Rising Unemployment and the High Street

For many people, a recession means that their jobs may be at risk. In December 2008, the number of people in the US who were unemployed reached the highest level since 1993. In the last part of 2008, over 2 million Americans lost their jobs. In Britain, the number of unemployed people rose during 2008 to just under 2 million. This was the highest figure since 1997. Most experts agree that unemployment will rise around the world throughout the recession.

One of the consequences of rising joblessness is that many businesses have found themselves in trouble as people spend less. This is most obvious when chains of shops close. In Britain, shops such as Woolworths have closed their doors for the last time. In the US, the coffee store Starbucks announced that it would close 600 stores in 2009.

As the recession began to spread, people became reluctant to spend money. Many shops have offered huge cuts in prices in order to get people to spend again.

'Fear has started to take over now. Since being made redundant it's become obvious that the jobs aren't out there. And what jobs there are, an awful lot of people are applying for them.'

Mike Kirkham-Jones, unemployed since August 2008

The Stock Markets React

One of the ways that people can tell how healthy their economy is to see how the stock markets are performing. When the economy is doing well, then people are more likely to buy shares in companies. This is because if companies make bigger profits then shareholders will have a bigger share of that profit. Shareholders will also make money if they sell their shares at a higher price than they originally paid. When an economy starts to do badly, then shareholders are less keen to buy shares and will try to sell what they have. This causes the value of shares to fall.

A trader watches share prices fall on an electronic board.

Bears and Bulls

When stock markets are doing well then it is described as a 'bull market'. If stock markets are doing badly then it is often called a 'bear market'. The first time that the phrase 'bear market' was used in 2008 was on 21 January. Stock markets around the world reacted to continuing bad economic news with heavy falls in the value of shares. It was the biggest fall since 2001. The next day, the US Federal Reserve cut their interest rates and stock markets recovered. On 16 September, there were heavy falls on stock markets as US unemployment figures jumped up. The companies that were hardest hit were also those that were suffering under the credit crunch, such as banks and house-building companies.

'The turmoil in financial markets and the funding pressures on financial firms pose a significant threat to economic growth. The last decade has shown that

bursting bubbles

can be an extraordinarily dangerous and costly phenomenon for the US economy.'

Ben Bernanke, chairman of the Federal Reserve

There were criticisms of the way that the stock markets have reacted to bad economic news. Do you think it is inevitable that stock markets will react in this way or do you think traders have taken advantage of a difficult situation.

THOUGHT BOX

There was another record fall on 29 September. The House of Representatives in the USA had just rejected President Bush's rescue package for the struggling banks. The US stock market was faced with the biggest one-day fall in its history. The week starting 6 October has been called the 'Black Week', because stock markets all over the world fell heavily every day. On 24 October, stock markets around the world suffered another sharp fall. Charles Bean, the deputy governor of the Bank of England, said that this was 'the largest financial crisis of its kind in human history'.

Panic Selling

Many people have suggested that stock markets around the world have over-reacted to bad economic news. When something such as higher unemployment figures are announced, then shares in some companies drop slightly. Other shareholders see that shares are being sold and they panic. They decide to quickly sell their shares as well so that they do not make too much of a loss. Suddenly stock markets start to crash even though there is no real reason for it to happen.

Share prices are displayed on the sides of buildings in Times Square in New York.

Cars Feel the Pinch

In a recession, people are far more careful about how they spend their money and will think twice before making a big purchase of any kind. Other than housing, one of the biggest purchases that anybody makes is a car, especially a new car. Throughout 2008, car industries around the world saw their sales fall. Part of the reason for this was the very high price of fuel for much of 2008. Larger cars that use more petrol were especially hit as the world entered recession.

Car factories around the world have announced that they will be losing workers or are cutting down the number of hours that their workers can work.

Falling Sales

Nearly every car manufacturer around the world has seen large falls in sales and many of them have begun to cut back on their workforce in order to stay in profit. In January 2009, the Japanese car maker Nissan said that they were going to cut over 1,000 jobs at their Sunderland factory in Britain. The French car company Peugeot Citroen announced in November 2008 that it was going to cut its workforce by 2,500. In Japan, Mazda and Isuzu are cutting the number of workers by over 3,000. Some car companies in Germany are not getting rid of workers but are cutting the hours they can work or have closed the factories for a few months at a time.

THOUGHT BOX

President Bush said that in normal circumstances he would allow companies to fail. Do you think exceptional circumstances should mean it is ok to intervene in the market to protect businesses?

The Big Three

The car industry in the USA centres around the Big Three companies of General Motors (GM), Ford and Chrysler. All of them are based in the city of Detroit. In November 2008, all three companies announced that they had suffered big losses over the past year. This was not just because of general economic problems. Fuel-efficient cars were becoming more popular in the USA. The Big Three were still making cars that use a lot of fuel.

In December 2008, the bosses of the Big Three went to the US Congress for financial help but their pleas were rejected. Some members of the US government wanted the unions to accept wage cuts for car workers. When the unions refused, Congress decided not to help. In the end, President Bush had to come forward with his own rescue plan for the US car industry. He announced that he was going to take US$17.4 billion from the US$700 billion rescue package for the banking industry. Ford decided not to take any money, but General Motors took US$9.4 billion and Chrysler took US$4 billion.

Car sales have fallen around the world. Larger cars that use a lot of fuel have been badly hit and many car sellers have had to offer large discounts.

'This action will help to **preserve many jobs** and support the continued operation of GM and the many suppliers, dealers and small businesses across the country that depend on our company.'

Rick Wagoner, the boss of GM, thanking President Bush for the financial help

China and the Credit Crunch

After the USA, the largest economy in the world is the People's Republic of China. During the 1990s and the first years of the 21st century, China experienced an economic growth that has been both envied and feared by other countries. The incomes of Chinese people have grown at about 10 per cent every year. The Chinese economy has depended on demand for goods from Europe and the USA. As the recession spread around the world, then China was affected as well.

'It is useful to remember that this is the first time...in which China's economy has become sufficiently involved with other economies that troubles in the USA, Europe and Japan would affect China. Welcome, Beijing, to the **rough and tumble** of the globally competitive marketplace.'

Donald Straszheim, an expert on the Chinese economy

The Workshop of the World

China has become one of the most important manufacturing countries in the whole world. Out of the top 500 manufacturing companies in the world about 400 have factories in China. China builds over 30 per cent of the world's computers, over 60 per cent of microwave ovens and 40 per cent of all televisions. On top of that, half of all the clothes made in the world are made in China. In China itself, demand for luxury Western goods such as perfume or champagne has grown fast.

Chinese workers produce over half of all the clothes made in the world.

Reacting to the Credit Crunch

Nearly 50 per cent of all China's exports go to the USA, Europe and Japan. As these three economies began to shrink, so demand for Chinese goods began to fall slightly. Economic growth fell to about 8 per cent. This meant that China is nowhere near entering a recession itself, but the growth that it had taken for granted had begun to slow down. The rise in food prices, particularly in rice, also affected the Chinese economy.

On 9 November 2008, the Chinese government announced that it was putting forward a stimulus package that looked similar to the rescue packages created by other governments. Over 4 trillion yuan (about US$586 billion) was going to be invested in key areas such as housing, transport, health and education, environment and tax cuts. When the package was announced, stock markets around the world reacted positively and share prices went up. Many people feel that it will be the Chinese consumer that will eventually pull the world out of recession.

Goods made in China are shipped all over the world in massive countainer ships such as this one.

THOUGHT BOX

Do you think that China will become even more powerful as its main competitors go into recession, while China will just have slightly slower economic growth?

35

Iceland and the Credit Crunch

In the North Atlantic Ocean lies the small and thinly-populated island of Iceland. It has a population of about 300,000 and most people live in the capital city of Reykjavik. For many years, Icelandic people have enjoyed one of the highest standards of living in the world. Originally fishing was the main industry, but as this became less important, Iceland came to rely on the banking and financial industries for its wealth. When the credit crunch arrived, Iceland was particularly hard hit.

The Growth in Banking

At the start of 2008, Iceland seemed to be enjoying a period of growing prosperity. The central bank in Iceland kept interest rates high. This encouraged foreigners to invest their money in Iceland. Both Icelandic and foreign savers put

As the Icelandic economy began to suffer there were regular protests in Reykjavik against the Icelandic government.

'It is ridiculous, really, the way Icelanders got used to having lots of things, to **being rich on borrowed money.** We are going to change our diet, we are going to shop differently, we are only going to use cash, no cards. The worst thing is we just don't know what is coming.'

Lara Omarsdottir, an Icelandic woman, expresses her shock after both she and her partner lost their jobs

their money in Icelandic banks because savings attracted a high interest rate. Icelandic banks also began to buy up debts from foreign banks. The three main banks grew so large that together they were ten times larger than the rest of the Icelandic economy.

The Credit Crunch Arrives

In the summer of 2008, the crisis in the banking world meant that Iceland's banks suddenly found themselves in trouble. They had a lot of foreign debts that they were having great difficulty paying off. In the end, the Icelandic government had to nationalise the three largest Icelandic banks in order to stop them from collapsing. The financial crisis was so great that in November 2008, the Icelandic government was forced to borrow money from the International Monetary Fund (IMF). This was the first time that a Western

European country has had to take such a loan since 1976. Many British savers had put money into Icelandic banks. The collapse in Icelandic banks meant that they could not repay any of this money. This led to the British government using special laws to try and get British money back.

The Icelandic Economy

In the last part of 2008, the Icelandic economy began to enter a deep recession. Unemployment tripled between August and November 2008. The IMF warned that the Icelandic economy will shrink by 10 per cent in 2009. The Icelandic Krona lost a lot of its value against other currencies. This made foreign goods much more expensive in Iceland. The stock market also had to be closed for two days in October 2008, to stop shares in Icelandic companies from collapsing completely.

Geir Haarde was Prime Minister until January 2009. Under his leadership Iceland entered one of the most turbulent periods of its history.

Do you think that the rest of the world should be concerned about Iceland's economic problems? Do you think these problems could happen elsewhere in the world?

THOUGHT BOX

Parallels — The Wall Street Crash

Although the credit crunch and the recession have come about because of what happened in the USA at a particular time, many people look back to previous economic troubles to see if any lessons can be learned. The one period that appears to have some similarities with what is happening today is the Wall Street Crash of 1929 and the Great Depression of the 1930s.

The Wall Street Crash

During the middle years of the 1920s, the US stock market enjoyed a boom period. Shares increased in value by over 500 per cent in this period. This was much higher than growth in the US economy. People were simply buying shares and selling them almost immediately at a higher price. It seemed that the rises would go on forever. Of course, they did not. The crash started on Thursday 24 October 1929. On the next Monday and Tuesday, the stock market collapsed completely. Every one of these three days saw a record loss on the stock market. Things continued to slide downwards at a slower pace until 1931. It was not until 1954 that the stock market returned to its 1929 levels.

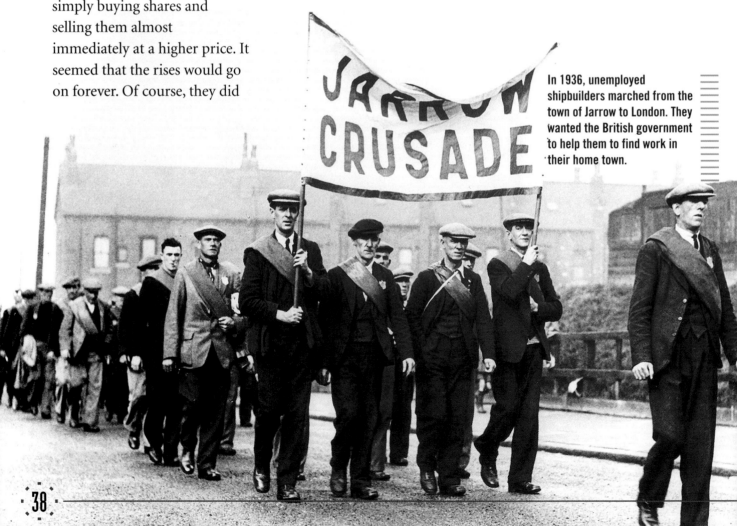

In 1936, unemployed shipbuilders marched from the town of Jarrow to London. They wanted the British government to help them to find work in their home town.

THOUGHT BOX

What similarities and differences are there between the Wall Street Crash and Great Depression and the Credit Crunch and the coming recession?

This line of statues commemorates the mass unemployment that was suffered by countries all over the world during the Great Depression of the 1930s.

The Great Depression of 1929

The Wall Street Crash was one of the causes of the Great Depression. Just like during the credit crunch, banks in the USA and in Europe began to get into trouble and were having difficulties paying off their debts. This sparked a 'run on the bank' similar to that of Northern Rock (see page 17). Customers panicked and tried to take their money out of the banks. Unemployment around the world began to climb steadily. In the USA it reached its peak in 1933, with an unemployment rate of 25 per cent.

Road to Recovery

In 1932, Franklin D. Roosevelt became US President of the United States. He started what is known as the New Deal. He used government money to try and create new jobs for Americans. However, while it helped some people, the New Deal did not pull the US economy out of depression. It was only with start of World War II in 1939, when governments around the world began to start spending money on a large scale, that the Great Depression began to recede.

'Yes. we are on the way back — not by mere chance, not by a turn of the cycle. We are coming back more soundly than ever before because we planned it that way, and don't let anybody tell you differently.'

President Franklin D. Roosevelt speaking in 1935

The Future

Predicting what will happen in the future is always going to be risky. At the start of 2007, very few people would have predicted the credit crunch and the recession that would come with it. Yet now it is easy to look back and to see that it was going to happen. Nevertheless, some have tried to look into the future and come up with forecasts for the world economy in 2009 and 2010.

The headquarters of the World Bank. It is based in Washington DC.

The World Bank Forecasts

The World Bank believes that the global recession that started in 2008 is set to continue, and that any recovery will not begin until 2010. It does not see any more crashes in house prices or the value of shares on the stock market. However, it does believe that there will be a steady rise in unemployment and further falls in house prices and in the price of goods generally.

The World Bank has warned that if the various rescue packages put together by different governments do not succeed, then there is a strong possibility of a deep and long recession which may last for many years.

Barack Obama became US President in January 2009. He has promised to pull the American economy out of recession through tax cuts and government spending.

Unemployment Continues to Rise

The respected Chartered Institute of Personnel and Development has said that the recession in Britain will deepen and that unemployment will reach 3 million. This would be the worst unemployment figure for 20 years. Most economic commentators believe that unemployment will also carry on rising in the USA. Alan Greenspan, former Chairman of the Federal Reserve, has said that the best to hope for is that the recession will be less severe than others have predicted.

The Obama Rescue Plan

On 9 January 2009, President Barack Obama outlined his plan for helping the US economy to recover. He pledged that government money would be spent on saving or creating 3 million jobs through investing in 'green' technologies and improving America's schools and universities. There will also be tax cuts so that Americans have more money to spend. It may be several years before any benefits of this plan will be seen.

'It is time to set a new course for this economy, and that change must begin now...For every day we wait or point fingers or drag our feet, more Americans will lose their jobs. More families will lose their savings. More dreams will be deferred and denied. And our nation will sink deeper into a crisis that, at some point, we may not be able to reverse.'

US President Barack Obama announcing his rescue package for the US economy in January 2009

Glossary

Bad Debt Sometimes called Toxic Debts. These are debts that have little chance of ever being paid back.

Bear Market When the value of shares on stock markets falls rapidly.

Bull Market When the value of shares on stock markets rises rapidly.

Central Bank A bank that is either owned by the government or works for the government. It regulates financial institutions and lends money to other banks.

Congress Part of the US government.

Credit A way of buying something that will be paid for in the future. This is normally done over an agreed period of time.

Credit Crunch Also known as a credit crisis. This is when banks are unwilling to lend money either to other banks or to other businesses or individuals.

Credit Rating A score based on whether a business or individual is more or less likely to be able to pay back a loan.

Depression A much deeper and longer-lasting recession.

Economic Cycle When an economy goes from doing well to doing badly and then gradually going back to doing well again.

Foreclosure When a mortgage lender takes back a property because the borrower is unable to pay the mortgage.

Free-Market Economy When an economy has few rules and regulations that may have an effect on how they perform.

House of Representatives Part of the United States government.

Housing Bubble When the price of properties grows very fast.

Inflation A rise in prices.

Interest Extra money that is paid by a borrower to a bank or another financial institution that lends money. It is calculated as a percentage of the original loan.

International Monetary Fund (IMF) A United Nations agency to promote trade by increasing the exchange stability of the major currencies.

Liquidity Crisis When banks will not lend money to other banks. This also means that they cannot borrow from other banks either.

Mortgage A loan of money in order to buy a property. It is paid back over a number of years and has an interest rate attached to it.

Nationalisation When a business is taken over by the government.

Negative Equity When the value of a property falls below the amount of money that was borrowed to buy it.

Recession When an economy stops growing and starts shrinking instead for two successive quarters.

Repossession When a mortgage lender takes back a property because the borrower is unable to pay the mortgage.

Share A part of a company that is owned by a shareholder and bought on the Stock Market.

Shareholder Someone who owns shares in a company.

Short Selling This is when somebody makes money from falling share values. Shares are borrowed from a shareholder and then sold at a high price. When the price falls then the shares are bought back and the profits divided between the borrower and the original owner of the shares.

Stock Market Sometimes called a Stock Exchange. A place where shares in companies are bought and sold.

Sub-Prime Lending Lending money to people who may not be able to pay back the loans.

Unemployment Being out of work.

World Bank An international organisation that was formed in 1945 to help economies that are struggling.

Weblinks

http://www.federalreserveeducation.org/FRED
Resources for schools created by the Federal Reserve.

http://www.bankofengland.co.uk/education/index.htm
Resources for schools created by the Bank of England.

http://news.bbc.co.uk/1/hi/business/7521250.stm
A timeline on the credit crunch created by the BBC.

Note to parents and teachers:
Every effort has been made by the Publishers to ensure that these websites are suitable for children, that they are of the highest educational value, and that they contain no inappropriate or offensive material. However, because of the nature of the Internet, it is impossible to guarantee that the contents of these sites will not be altered. We strongly advise that Internet access is supervised by a responsible adult.

Index